ALASKA

twenty poems and a journal

ALASKA
twenty poems and a journal

by Brod Bagert

with drawings by Stephen Morillo

JULIAHOUSE PUBLISHING CO.
P.O. Box 24224
New Orleans, Louisiana 70184
Library of Congress Catalog Card No. 88-081622
ISBN 0-9614228-3-1
Printed in the United States of America

Designed by Nick Marinello

Dedicated to John David
the two-year-old of my 40th year

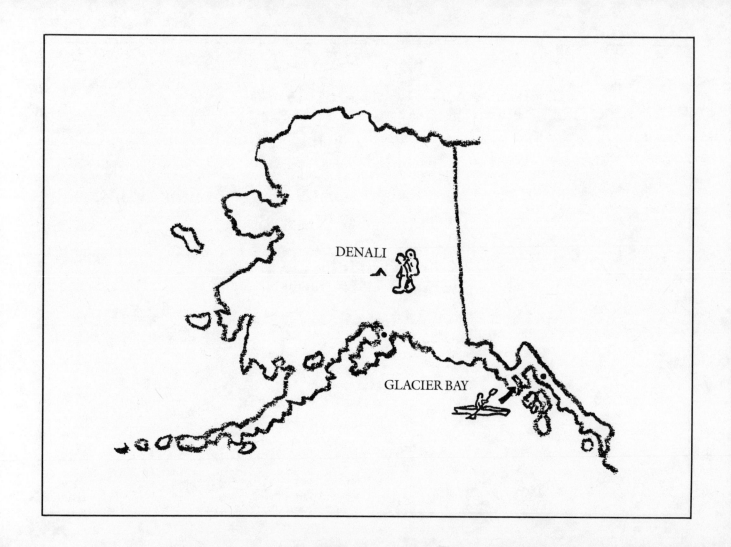

DENALI

GLACIER BAY

Contents

Prologue

This book is the result of a conversation at a wedding in New Orleans — 4,000 miles from Alaska. As I bemoaned the sedentary life of the 20th century urban professional, fate carried my remarks to the ears of Mike Vales, the nephew of my wife's sister's husband. He suggested a backpacking excursion to Alaska. And so it was that several months later I found myself at a depot in the city of Anchorage, ticket in hand, ready for a ride on the Alaskan railroad.

I have since learned that fate had little to do with the events of that summer. Had I commented on the weather, Mike Vales would have suggested a trip to Alaska. Had I complained of mid-life burnout, he would have recommended Alaska. The National Debt? Alaska. He was determined. It was a veritable kidnapping.

This book, then, tells the story of a middle-aged lawyer in the wilds of the Arctic. Most of it was written at night in a tent by a moderately obese 38-year-old who had spent the day acting like a teenager. I had intended to publish only the poems, but have included the journal at the urging of the artist, Steve Morillo. It remains largely unedited and is offered not for literary value, but as a backdrop against which to read the poems.

A word about the poems. They can be read separately or together, like footprints on a path. The drawings which accompany the poems are intended to give you the kind of information that a live audience derives from the voice and facial expression of a performer. They simply convey a visual sense of the mood of each poem — the props for the stage on which you supply the performance.

And so, without further explanation, "Let us go then, you and I..."

ACT ONE

SUMMER TUNDRA

Denali is the treeless green of quiet spirits, a shaft in time where the modern heart beats with the pulse of primeval ancestors.

Imagine yourself at the top of a small mountain. It is the evening of a day on which the sun will never set. In the distance, above the clouds, the alpine peak of Denali is a pyramid of floating white. Be small... breathe softly... listen for the voice of the mountain.

Big Talk

Well it says here
That a grizzly will eat wild flowers.
Now ain't that a pretty picture,
A thousand pounds of bear
Twelve feet tall
Stuffed to a smile with wild flowers.

I lean back in my chair,
Hike my boots up on the table,
And in the womb of a foot-thick log lodge
Laugh at the lord of the tundra.

13

Solitary Talisman

The emergency exit shrinks
In a cloud of dust,
The bus sinks down and around the hill,
The drone of engine fades…
And I am alone in the wilderness…
Alone in this world of mountain kings…
Alone…
Armed only with the tinkle of a bear bell.

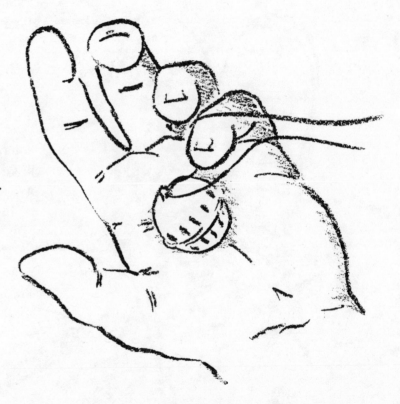

Necessities
(Four Miles Out)

I will not wear two pair of shorts,
I do not need the extra sweater
And one towel would have been sufficient . . .
But I brought them anyway,
I stuffed them in my pack,
And now I hate each extra ounce
I carry on my back.

Odor of Man

Out three days
With earth and open air,
As my flesh becomes the smell
Man used to be,
I begin to understand
Why the beasts of the land
Once ran from the likes of me.

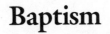

Baptism

I have shed two layers of clothing
And should be shivering
In this bright chill of arctic summer night
But I have bathed in the cold
Of a snow-fed stream,
And now, somehow, the arctic air
Is warmer than it seemed.

17

Tundra Campsite

We lived here last night,
There were tents
And clothes
And cooking stoves
But with the rising of the sun
It is gone.
We leave little behind,
Wild flowers
Sunshine
And our dreams
Like dew.

Follow the Caribou

It was an easy walk across the mountain,
We carried only day packs
Ate snow as we climbed
And were certain of the paths we chose,
For a caribou had come this way before us
And in the wisdom of his tracks
There was peace in the way of our crossing.

Lost Spectacles

I lost my glasses on the mountain.
Soon I will return to the glass tower,
I will ride the elevator to the 38th floor,
And I will reside again inside walls
Where framed documents certify who I am...
But when thunder threatens southern winter rain
I will remember the glasses I left behind,
And they will be here still...
Somewhere on the slopes of Mount Thoro...
Cold and blind beneath the snow.

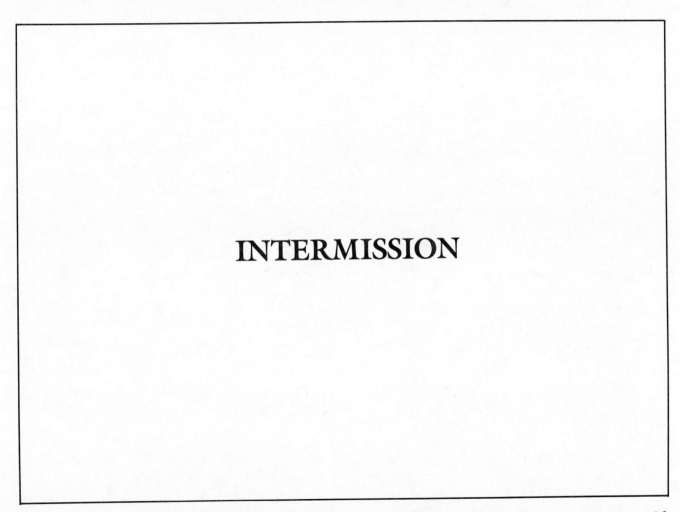

INTERMISSION

Lotus Eater
(To Politics)

It began as harmless conversation
About the choreography of candidate debate,
Words that speak in tongues,
The poetry of a thirty-second lie…
And I am at it again,
A dreamer in this den
Of smoke and yellow fame,
Where everyone smiles
And no one speaks my name.

25

The Gustavus Inn

It's so very nice in here.
They bring us meals
Give us bicycles to ride
And let us play anywhere on the island.
But in the morning we must make our own beds,
Imagine that,
We make our very own beds.

ACT TWO

WATER, ROCK AND ICE

It is the misty bare rock mountain roost of rowdy seabirds — a summer playground for whales — and yet — the spirit groans in Glacier Bay as great dinosaur bones of ice crack asunder and thunder down into a hungry sea.

Follow me with caution, beware ripples on the water and resist the blue glass beauty of ice, for I have looked into the face of the glacier and there is cold in the calling of her frozen heart.

Birds and Men

I crouched in a kayak
Amidst floating slabs of glacial ice,
The mist cleared,
And, as if risen from the sea,
There appeared before me
A great wall of a mountain.

HELLO !
And the mountain called back …
HELLO… HELLO…

I AM HERE !
And the rock laughed.
I AM HERE… HERE…

And there was silence,
As canvas skin on wooden frame
Bobbed with the swell of waves,
And seabird children of the rock
Chose refuge in the sky.

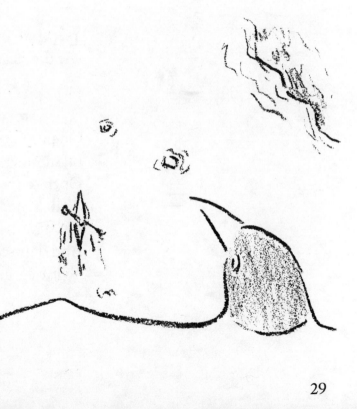

Fireweed
(At the edge of ice flow)

How precariously you cling
To the stones of this moraine,
Oh purple blossom child
Of summer sun and rain,
Open to the wind
And do not fear its sting,
For snow soon comes to bury you
And only seed will ferry you
To live again in spring.

Time Tea and Fire

I brewed this cup of tea
With water melted
From the ice of a glacier,
Frozen these fifty thousand years…
Warm again
In the belly of a man.

Love Song of a Hollofil Sleeping Bag

I am alone
And I am cold.
Come to me.
Unzip me.
Fill me with the warmth of your body.

From the dark and cold of a rocky shore
I can resist her call no more.

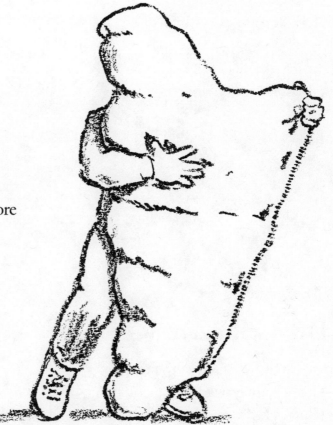

Dry Cell Battery

I write by flashlight in the dark
The battery grows weak
There is little time to speak

Night Invader

Under power of propeller
It prowls the fjord.
It must have seen my tent on the shore,
The curious green glow of inner-lit nylon,
For it comes.
It crawls across the water.
It snarls across the bay.
With one bright light
It licks the night away.

Coyote Nights

There is thunder in the distance
As ice tumbles into the sea,
Raindrops cry on the fly of my tent,
A crevasse splits inside me,
And it begins…
A growl that bulges at the zipper of my soul,
A silent howl,
A longing to unfold
To the open curve of a waxing crescent moon,
To fill the hollow of the moon.

Song of the Moth

I floated in the face of the glacier
Toward crystal cliffs of frozen blue,
I paddled more slowly at first
Then not at all
For as turquoise water turned to ash
I began to understand what place this was,
This place . . . where ice pounds into the sea . . .
This cold place
Whose voice now chants inside me
In rhythm with each stroke
As I pull faster and faster from her reach . . .

> *Paddle paddle far away*
> *Spew white foam and salt sea spray*
> *Run until the final day*
> *When closer you will come again*
> *Child of ice come home to stay.*

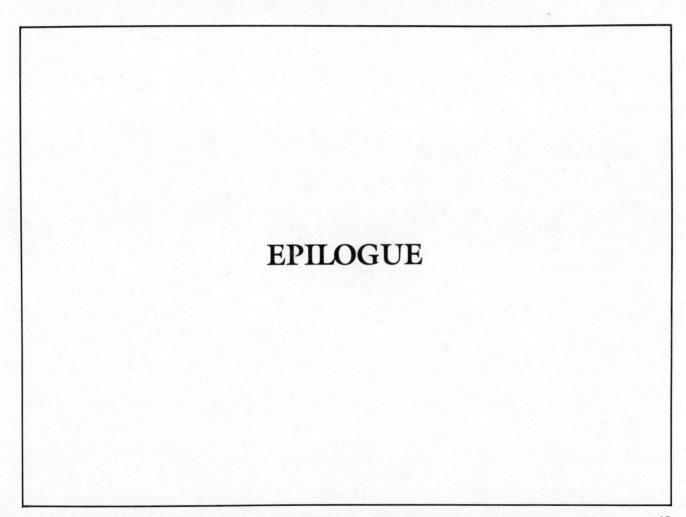

EPILOGUE

The Hook

Hot water,
The smell of soap,
Clean white sheets
And sleep.
My body gleeeeams!
The snow-fed river
Is a shiver in my dreams.

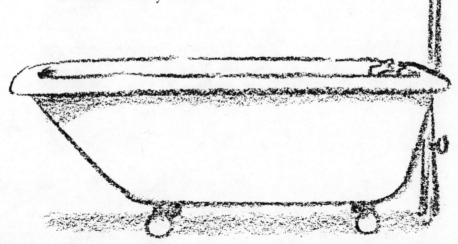

Facing It

Tomorrow I go back.
Our flight will board by rows,
They will serve honey-roasted peanuts,
My backpack will float toward me
On a conveyor belt,
And I will be home again,
Wife… work…children…
The wilderness of Alaska is a boy's game
After all it's not Peru…
Oh I've heard wonderful things about Peru.
Jungle… shrunken heads…
And llamas…
Real live llamas !

Journal

July 25–August 8, 1986

JULY 25

Afternoon. I have been in the air today for seven-and-a-half hours and have another hour to go before we reach Anchorage. I'm very tired. We will have flown about 4,500 miles. We crossed the entire American West. It is not real.

I left my watch in New Orleans. I was going to buy a cheap one for the trip. I don't think I will now. I'm beginning to like the sense of irresponsibility.

The Alaska Airlines flight crew is different from the crews of regular airlines. When they say hello and smile I get the feeling they mean it. Very casual, very relaxed. Welcome to Alaska.

I just read Ben Johnson's poem on the death of his seven-year-old son. There is a beautiful line — "Here doth lie Ben Johnson his best piece of poetry." It is very sad. All his words are little compared to his love for his son. It is gentle and restrained and powerful.

I already miss Debby and the kids. I suspect the real adventure of this trip will not be mountains and whales. I'm afraid it will be a meeting with loneliness. What a wimp!

I am very tired.

JULY 27

We have pitched camp near the lodge just inside the entrance to Denali. Tomorrow we head for the back country. Today I read a piece on "bear safety" in the park newspaper. "If confronted by a grizzly bear, do not run. Face the creature instead, hold your arms up over your head and speak to the bear in a stern voice…" OK…

It is after midnight and I am writing this inside my tent by natural light. I begin to suspect that sleep habits are a function of darkness. It does not seem like bedtime.

As I crawled in my sleeping bag I was suddenly awash in a wave of nostalgia. No giggles or complaints. No sibling rivalry. I begin to understand how much the family is part of my identity. I feel awkward, as if I'm going through an act. That is not to say it's not fun, because it is. But it's awkward.

The train ride up was an event in itself. Mt. McKinley looming beautiful in the distance, harmonica music and a songfest in the car, lots of happy golden-agers singing *Amazing Grace*. A few of them took pictures of Mike and me. They posed with us as if we were great mountain men or something. Two city boys from the flats of Louisiana dress the part, and *presto* — mountain men. It must be the beard.

JULY 28

Well, today was quite a day. I rode a bus for three hours on a hairpin mountain road — saw four grizzly bears on the way — got out in the middle of nowhere and walked into the mountains until I couldn't take another step. I pitched camp, crawled 200 yards away, cooked and ate dinner, crept and photographed a caribou and packed my food away in bear-proof containers. (The land is tundra and has no trees.) Refreshed and nourished and spurred on by abundant light, I then climbed a giant hill that a guy from Louisiana has the right to call a mountain and watched what should have been a sunset. It wasn't! Instead, a large orange sun angled across the western sky, refusing to go down.

From the mountaintop I spotted a pond about a thousand feet below me, climbed down and maintained the family ritual of an ice-water dip. Until that time I had worn a long underwear top, a wool shirt, an insulated vest, and an all-weather parka. That was 90 minutes ago and all I've worn since then is a wool shirt. It is amazing. An ice-cold swim makes chilly air warm.

I found a little trickle of a snow-fed stream and filter-pumped my bottles full. I've learned that I drink a lot of water.

I am now in bed (or bag), teeth brushed, tent organized, and as I write these words it occurs to me that a grizzly could be lumbering along outside the tent and I would never know it. At least, I hope I'd never know it.

Getting in my sleeping bag, I began to get leg cramps. I don't know if I'm losing weight, but if I'm not it must be a miraculous preservation of obesity induced by the will of some mischievous god. I am tired. It's about 11 p.m. and it is still daylight, and this is the craziest damn place in the world.

I finally started to relax today. I don't feel like talking much. My mind is mostly shut down. Usually, I see things, figure out what they mean, and draw analogies to everything else under the sun. I can tell I am relaxed today — I just observe events. I feel like one of the bears I saw today. He sat on the tundra, ate wild flowers, and rolled in the sun.

JULY 29 If you find this book, please send it to my wife and four loving children. I don't think I'm gonna make it.

We packed up and down hills today for a good three miles, maybe four.

I am in camp now on what I thought was halfway up a 7000-foot mountain called Mount Thoro. I can hear a snow-fed stream rushing down to the river. I am sleeping with my pillow, backpack, two water bottles and all my clothes under my sleeping pad. Why, you ask? I am on a 15% grade, and would otherwise slide out the bottom of my tent and down this mountain. In using the words ''this mountain'' I have suppressed the desire to describe it with four-letter words. I climbed it today. I confess that objectively it was more of a hike, but for someone who fears heights it was a climb. I overcame my fear. I trudged, crawled and wallowed on my belly. The last 300 yards were a nightmare of mud at what seemed like an angle of 60 degrees, an impossible pile of little muddy gravel and patches of snow just deep enough to make sure you couldn't see your footing. Exhausted, frightened, and having eaten ten gallons of snow (very thirsty work), I made it to a wall just before the summit, a vertical rise of about 40 ft. composed entirely of large crumbly rocks (fathers of future mud and gravel).

At one point I held on with everything but my eyelashes. I was a matter of feet from the top and there was a rock just out of reach which would have taken me to the top. I probably could have made a tiny lunge and grabbed it. Instead, I struggled up a few more inches and tested with a gentle tug. Ah, sweet caution. It came loose and it was all I could do to keep it off to the side of me as it began its long tumble down the mountain.

I thought of Debby — at least the insurance would make her a very wealthy woman — the kids, and all the poetry I'd never get to write. It was, of course, the latter that knocked some sense into me.

On the way down, I simply lay on my stomach, dug the toe of each boot into the mud and plowed backward down the steep part, leaving behind two parallel furrows six inches deep to mark my ungainly retreat.

I practically ran down the rest of the way. What on the way up seemed breathtakingly steep, seemed now like a N.O. sidewalk by comparison to the insanity of the top.

So, today we backpacked for about three hours, and climbed for three hours. I am mush.

Got what I think will be some good photographs of a caribou. It went up the mountain ahead of us. We saw his tracks most of the way up. He seemed clever at choosing the course of least resistance. At one point the tracks solved a dilemma as to which way to go. We had grown to respect his wisdom and decided not to second-guess him.

I am absolutely fuzzy with fatigue. Consciousness is a burden. Actually, I have the urge to attend to one of nature's most fundamental calls but I don't have the energy. Besides, something has been stomping around outside the tent. I have been hearing noises for the last few minutes but I don't have the energy to look out. Actually, I don't want to know. It's a little like worrying about nuclear war. If it comes it comes.

If I don't get in the dark soon I'll go batty.

The last time I experienced darkness was when I woke up to catch the plane Saturday morning. I can't remember what day it is but I know that was a long time ago.

I wish Debby were here. Mike and I ate dinner on a plateau about 2,000 feet up overlooking a panorama of mountains and rivers, and sky that was spectacular — a visual version of Handel's "Alleluia Chorus." Maybe Debby and I can take the kids to Big Bend in Texas. I've just written the "Tundra Campsite" poem. I have the feeling that it will stay pretty much as is.

JULY 30

It is early afternoon. We are now in a campground at Wonder Lake. They call it that because the view is so beautiful. It is raining, however, and the only view I have is the inside of my tent. Even this, however, is a blessing. I'm worn out and need the rest.

This morning we hiked down from "Asshole Mountain" (you remember the one), crossed the river and hiked out to the road. Somewhere along the way I lost my glasses. I went back without a pack and tried to find them, but no luck. On the way out, I found a grizzly track. It was on a sandy rise in the bed of the river. It was a little longer than my foot. In width, it was four times that of mine. I could even see the claw marks.

We ate lunch on the road and caught the bus to Wonder Lake. There were a bunch of kids on a teen tour. They looked bored as hell so I got my harmonica out and got 'em all singing. They even sang "God Bless America." I told them that the difference between my generation and theirs is that they sang it. In the 'sixties they would have booed and sung some Joan Baez protest song instead.

Well, here we are in Wonder Lake. The rain taps steadily on the tent fly and I am happy for the rest. Every muscle in my body is depleted.

I wonder if I lost my glasses on purpose.

Perhaps my unconscious is surreptitiously shedding the remnants of civilization. Perhaps this will be a *Call of the Wild* transformation. After all, this is the kind of country it happened in.

Midnight. Call of the wild, my heinie. I just took a hot shower and I'm nestled on a real mattress between clean sheets and I am glad to be out of the rain. Lots has happened since the last entry. I slept, read from *Norton's Anthology of Poetry*, wrote the Caribou poem, slept some more and rewrote "Fireweed" into something decent. Slept some more, ate banana chips and pita bread, slept some more. Did I say, "The rain tapped steadily on the tent fly and I am happy for the rest?" After four hours of steady tapping in a tent the size of a coffin, funny stuff starts happening. It was getting moist inside. Would it stay dry? Would my down sleeping bag get wet? Would I die of exposure before morning and after all didn't I already feel a cold coming on — a little chestiness, maybe?

Next thing I know I'm walking in the rain

for fun. I saw a guy with an identical rain suit and told him how funny he looked. I walked to the lake and on the way a park bus splashed water on me waist-high. Did I say bus? Bus, as in a ride back to civilization — and doesn't that mean dryness?

Well, there you have it. Fifteen minutes to break camp, a scramble to catch the last bus without a second to spare, and five hours of wet mountain roads (I seem to have lost my fear of heights).

On the way, I wrote ''Talisman'' and ''Odor of Man.'' The latter is OK, but so far doesn't seem to work. I met a very nice young couple who live in Anchorage. The warmth of their love for each other made me very homesick for Debby. (That's interesting — New Orleans does not show up as home, Debby does. Day after tomorrow will be 16 years. Good life.)

Well, after one hundred and ninety-seven stops to look at moose, mountain sheep, caribou herds, and little funky birds that look like road chickens (but are in fact ptarmigan, the Alaskan State Bird and very beautiful at that), we finally arrived back at the Denali Lodge, which was full. But who will question destiny. Joyce — a very nice lady ''married 23 years and all but the last 16 were good,'' who used to drive a semi in Minnesota, and who moved to Alaska for reasons not specified — Joyce suggested we catch her midnight bus to the Chalet where there was one room left, which we did and here we are in Paradise. I am slain in the spirit of civilization! Amen.

JULY 31

I have always wanted to eat a fine meal on a train. So here I am: fresh flowers on a white linen tablecloth and the Alaskan landscape passing by the window of the dining car.

I grow fonder and fonder of old T.S. Eliot. I read ''Prufrock'' and ''Preludes'' again today. Great stuff.

I have found the secret to happiness and it is there for anyone to experience. Spend three days in the wild, come in out of the cold and rain to a nice warm hotel room, take a hot bath, and sleep for nine hours between clean, white, dry sheets. It is heaven, the same heaven we live every day and take for granted.

The food is good. Green salad, jambalaya(!), stuffed fish, and broccoli.

There is so much about the camping that I haven't said. We saw a golden eagle…

Oh! Today we met a couple who camped on the west side of Mt. Thoro on Tuesday evening, the same time we climbed the east side. They told us there was a grizzly just below the top, which means we were all up there together: Mike, me and the bear. I'm glad I didn't see him. I might have grown the wings of man.

The rivers here are real rivers. They run, have rocks, and vary in volume of water with conditions. Our Mississippi is so much river we can no longer feel the soul of River in it. I see here the "river of a mountain," watch it swell with the morning's rain and I know River. The Mississippi is the "river of a continent." My imagination is not big enough to know River in it.

I am mellow. I feel as though I am part of the train, wobbling along, rocking. I feel as though I'm in hibernation, rebuilding stores of energy for the next part of the trip. Glaciers! Whales! What will it really be like?

AUG. 1

Today has been a weird day. We returned to civilization and the gods of organized society punished me for having had so much fun. (That really is quite a bit too dramatic.)

The flight to Juneau was nothing short of spectacular. Ice fields, coastal mountains and incredible glaciers. When we got to Juneau, the weather was bad and we couldn't land.

I feel so awkward writing this. I'm not in touch with my feelings; I'm going through the motions, and I have no enthusiasm for it.

The long and the short of it is that we were routed to a place called Sitka. We sat in the airport for about two hours. I met Fran Ulmer, former mayor of Juneau, who is running for the Alaska legislature. I think she should run for governor but she denies the ambition.

We started talking politics and one thing led to another, and the next thing I knew I was in her office writing a speech for her.

I can't believe it. I spent the afternoon tapping into the opinion pulse of Juneau and I feel like Mr. Spock when he did the Vulcan mind-lock (or whatever) with the mineral monster and felt all its pain.

I feel depressed and confused. None of this should reflect negatively on Fran — who seems in every respect sincere and well intentioned, and who is clearly a person of considerable talent. This should tell me something about me and politics.

I'm washing my clothes, everything is dirty.

Listen to me. It's mid-vacation blues, and here is the real problem. Today is our anniversary and I feel rotten about being away.

This is the truth. Suddenly, my handwriting got very clear and neat — as though my hand sighed with relief to have arrived at the truth.

I have no poetry in me tonight. I am as dry as tuna steak. See what I mean? Lousy metaphor. I'm not even sure it's true.

The first half of the trip is over. This notebook is almost full. I'll get a new one tomorrow.

AUG. 2

The Gustavus Inn is a trip. I want to start in three different places.

Physically it is a quaint little place — homey little bedrooms with curved walls reflecting the World War II quonset construction — but otherwise, country home all the way.

The food is wonderful.

The surrounding area, but for the Christmas trees, could be rural Mississippi in November.

The people at the inn are amazing. There is one unifying characteristic about my fellow guests at the Gustavus Inn which should be noted. We are all children. There are no grown-ups here. I'm not sure whether we left the grown-up in Juneau and permitted the child to emerge as a function of the circumstance or whether this place is a magnet for big kids. Whatever, this is a bunch of grown-up kids.

So far there are five people here who will be on the kayak trip. Besides Mike and I, there is a man named Carlos. He is an R.N., an avid kayaker, a long-bearded dreamer who this summer fulfilled a commitment to himself to spend his 30th birthday above the Arctic Circle. He believes whales are smarter than people, and views the loss of Eden as the dawn of the age of agriculture and the beginning of our problems — the point at which we took the path that would lead us from the life of purity still maintained by whales. This is an over-simplified statement of his thinking, which is interesting and not at all foolish.

There are two women, each the 180-degree, polar opposite of the other. Barbara is a pampered, jet-set, strikingly attractive sophisticate who keeps homes in both L.A. and London, and has a nine-week-old daughter whom she left in the care of a "nanny." She is a former Playmate of the Month and TV star. Brenda is a 40-year-old with two daughters aged seven and nine - divorced two years — who spent eight years in a hippie commune in Alabama, and is now studying some form of holistic healing. She took one look at me and said I crave sweets, can't stand heat, sleep with my feet out from the covers, that I'm a practical idealist and some other stuff I can't remember — and that the reason for all this is that I need sulphur in my diet and that I should give up coffee. She was right about enough of it that I'll try the sulphur, but the coffee is another issue.

Tonight I was a recluse. I've never felt like this before. I'm usually as forward as a three-month-old Labrador puppy. This should be interesting.

AUG. 3
Today was a laid-back day. Good food, nature hike, bike ride, a little reading and a nap.

We are briefed and readied for the kayak trip and I'm real excited.

Also, the group is shaping up real well. A doctor and his wife came in today, and a red-headed lady from Boston.

I have the feeling that tomorrow will begin the experience of a lifetime.

AUG. 4
It is almost midnight. It gets dark here so I am writing by flashlight.

We spent the afternoon floating on turquoise water, paddling through floating chunks of ice, with mountains rising up on either side shrouded in a continuous mist. It is beautiful.

On the way in this morning, fog kept the float plane within 100 ft. of the water, 25-50 ft. most of the way. The pilot dropped us off, promised to come back in four days and flew away. It is cold and wet but we are geared for it. Dampness is a constant threat. We have few clothes due to limited space in a kayak.

I have come to like the people I'm with very much.

AUG. 5
It is still raining. It is cold. It has rained nonstop now for two days. The only dry place I know of is the inside of my sleep-

ing bag, which is beginning to get damp.

I still have some dry clothes but I'm saving them for tomorrow. If it is still raining I'll go crazy if I don't have something dry.

Today we paddled to a glacier called "Majorie," seven miles there and seven miles back. The ice floes were so thick at one point, we went single file. We were watched constantly — a little head with black eyes pops into the periphery of vision and disappears beneath the surface the second I turn to look. Seals! They are everywhere.

The glacier was a sight to behold. The ice glows green in places as if it were enchanted, and in other spots it is black and muddy. We got to within 500 yards of the face. The water turned a milky grey, almost as if the glacier was warning us to stay away. And it was cold.

It is hard to explain. The cold was alive. It pumped out at you as though there were a great glacial heart that radiated cold, a cold that seemed to call you closer. But going closer is not wise, for every so often the glacier "calves" — a comparatively gentle metaphor. Tons of ice break off and tumble into the sea. The fall is so long and the perspective so distorted that the event appears to occur in slow motion. And, there is thunder. It rolls out and echoes between the mountains that wall the narrows of the fjord. I was impressed with a sense of awe, the equal of which I've never felt before. The spirit was not there. It was as though this was beyond life. It is as if the ice is death itself — terrible, cold, unrelenting and beautiful.

AUG. 6

Today was a great day. It started cold and wet. All my clothes were wet. I had one dry set of long underwear bottoms and one pair of dry socks, but I decided not to use them in case it did not stop raining. I feared I'd go insane on the last day unless I had something to look forward to. Well, things got better.

We paddled to Lampoon Glacier and went ashore at a place where land and ice meet in a way that permits a close view of the "Big G." Still breathtaking. We had lunch and were basking in the spell of nature when out of the mist there appeared a ship. It came ashore, lowered a gangplank from its bow and disgorged a herd of tourists who looked at us through camera lenses as though we were creatures from another planet. I will spare you the details of the insane burlesque by which Carlos and I entertained that entire sweet-smelling audience — we juggled stones, sang, danced, and performed feats of acrobatic "skill" — the audience applauded — we declined tips — they returned to the ship and left us on the shore, deaf to our pleas to be taken along.

We returned to our kayaks to discover that the tide had risen some 20 ft. and were thankful that trusted guide Greg had earlier insisted we haul our gear halfway up a hill that was now half under water.

We had a nice paddle to our new campsite.

We saw two Minke Whales (30 ft.long). I climbed another mountain, this time by myself. I saw ptarmigan on the way up, a pair with two babies. The mom was a hero. She displayed herself to distract me while the chicks slipped away in the opposite direction. I slid down about 600 yards of bumpy snow on the way down, ate a great meal, had a fire, sang songs and before the night ended, stars came out. They are the first stars I've seen in Alaska and they are all in the wrong places.

Tomorrow starts the journey home. I am ready to go. I miss Debby so much that I'm beginning to talk about her all the time.

Right now there is no sound but the distant roar of a mountain stream fed by melting snow. It is terribly romantic. I wish Debby were in the next sleeping bag, rather than snoring Michael.

I begin to wonder what John David looks like and how the other kids are.

Tomorrow night we lay over in Seattle.

Then Friday, it's home. I am ready.

AUG. 7

I am exhausted. The flight to Juneau was a quick hop and now we're on another plane, headed for Seattle.

The weather today was great. I am sunburned. Nothing new. A nice paddle, another glacier (Reed), a meal and lots of goofing around on a stone beach until the float plane arrived and took us out.

I feel like a person from another world, inside and out. The same dress that is comfortable and appropriate in the wild is conspicuous in the civilized world. The natural odor that protects people from bears is offensive here, and that wilderness sense of peace makes me feel downright vulnerable on a crowded airplane.

There are two nice kids in the seats next to me, ages 14 and 16. It makes me homesick. I realized this morning that I'm not scheduled to fly home till Saturday. That means a full day in Seattle. I'm gonna see if I can catch a red-eye out of Seattle and maybe fly in tonight.

Later. The Vance Hotel in Seattle has no air conditioning. Can you believe this? For the last three nights I've slept on the ground, in wet clothes, in the cold and miserable rain — and I complain that the Vance Hotel has no air conditioning. There truly seems to be no hope for humanity. What fickle creatures we are.

Maybe it's not so bad. Perhaps just I personally am hopeless, and not all my fellow human beings — but I doubt it. Maybe Mother Theresa — but the rest of us are bananas.

The bathtub in our room is the old-time design and is capable of harboring two simultaneous drowning victims. The knobs are porcelain and protrude from the side wall next to the tub. No overflow drain.

The sink, on the other hand, is a pissant addition of modern vintage, not worthy of further description. The guy who authorized that modernization probably was made manager.

It is 2:00 a.m. and I can't sleep. Mike is also awake. He turned on the light, and with intense surprise, concern and frustration, said, "I can't sleep!" He said it as though it were some great surprise. For the last 12 days we've slept in the wilderness. Even when we stayed in an inn, the population density of the surrounding hundred square miles was less than one person per mile. The loudest noise we've heard in the last 48 hours was the gas jet on a Coleman stove. We are on the second floor. Remember there is no air conditioning so the windows are open. Cities, I have just discovered, are very noisy places: cars, buses, sirens, trash-mashers on garbage trucks, horns, people laughing, 20 unidentifiable things that clatter — and a motorcycle with a muffler the size of a mosquito pecker. My ears are in pain… and this isn't even New York. "These little town shoes," my behind — give me some tundra.

But we are safe. Oh, yes. After all, on the tundra some senile bear might smell my toothpaste instead of my reeking body, and pay me a visit. He may, thereupon, go totally psycho and maul me, innocent in my sleeping bag. After all, it's happened maybe ten or twelve times in the last 50 years. So, at least now I'm safe, here in the city. (Have you noticed how cocky a guy can get about grizzly bears when there aren't any within a hundred miles?)

Mike is still awake — he examines his left thumbnail, has done so for the last five minutes, is still doing it. The vehicle that just drove by must be bigger than a train.

Mike wants to read "What's Special About Seattle" to me out loud. I decline and he, as always, cheerfully accepts the reaction. The kid is a saint. He shaved tonight and he looks like a new man. He carries a rosary with him, the same one his father carried with him throughout WW II as a foot soldier in the European theatre. I don't think it is an accident that of all his brothers, Mike got the rosary. He is a very special young man.

He is now complaining about the oil painting of a flower on the wall next to his bed and comparing it to a fragrant field of dwarf fireweed on the tundra of Denali. What can I say? "Go to sleep, Mike. Only bears and stuff get to live on the tundra all year round... and they don't get to eat all winter." He is placated. Mike likes to eat.

My hands are swollen. I think it's from the kayak paddle. I could hardly get my wedding ring back on this afternoon. I used as a lubricant some of that scented musk oil I bought on Orchard Street in New York. It's pretty strong stuff. A lady on the plane commented about how nice it was. Four days in a kayak without a bath, straight to a 727 and all she smelled was the oil. Bazooka oil!

It surprised me. We climbed out of the float plane, they gave us our backpacks (which had been stored, they don't fit in kayaks) and the first thing I did was put my wedding ring back on. I didn't even realize it until somebody commented. Next I checked the gifts I got for the kids and called home. If midlife travels of this kind are a search for identity, I think I've caught a glimpse of mine.

Mike puts on his shorts, a T-shirt, and walks out the door. Would that there were only bears to fear. Last night he could have walked away from camp for an hour and I could have yelled and he would have heard me.

He is back. The hotel management will not give us a different room. I am not surprised.

AUG. 8
Seattle is a nice place. It is very much like New Orleans: lots of seafood, a

waterfront area nicely developed, even a "French Market." It is not, however, as hot, as black, or as romantic.

I bought lots of junk and had a good time doing it.

Tomorrow we go home. There is nothing else in the whole world I'd rather do.

I met a man day before yesterday, on the flight from Juneau to Seattle. He'd spent three weeks on a glacier in Alaska. There is an ongoing study by his university, I believe in Idaho. There are a number of permanent outposts on the glacier. They are continuously in motion. The scholars climb in crevasses and learn about the climate of the Earth thousands of years ago. There is poetry in that. It's hard to write about a glacier. It's like writing about a whole world. If I could spend a week on a glacier I think I could get it.

The thing about a glacier is the cold — cold not all around but from a direction — cold with purpose, radiant cold — and just as radiant warmth from a fire speaks of safeness and light and life, the cold that radiates from the face of a glacier is the whisper of eternal darkness.

I have taken a liking to the idea of mountain climbing. I'm still a coward about heights. It scares the daylights out of me. But I like climbing anyway. There is a sense of purpose in climbing a mountain. The purpose is to get to the top. For the time it takes to accomplish that, there is no confusion. Life is simple. What other purpose is there, anyway? There are many, of course, and all good ones — but so is getting to the top of a pile of rocks. No better. No worse. Out of the fast lane and up the high road.

I haven't been to Idaho, North Dakota, and much of Canada and Latin America. Those places have lots of mountains. Maybe I'll do some climbing. Just think, my very own ice ax... and crampons... and carabineers. It is more than my childish and romantic heart can stand.

But for now, I want one thing. I want to see Debby at the airport at 2:30 p.m. tomorrow. I want to take her in my arms and I want to tell her I love her.

I feel terribly corny writing this entry. I want to hold back, but what I write is true and I should say it. I will write poetry on ice, I will climb mountains, and I will love my wife more than life itself. (I can't stand it.)

It is almost as though I am not myself without her. Indeed, I am not. I have an act. I do lots of conversation and perform a whole bunch of tricks. I can entertain groups. Good Lord, Carlos and I literally entertained a whole gawking boatload of tourists and their crew at Lampoon. Yet it seems that the me inside of me has become part of her.

She is strong, she is tender and she is beautiful. She is beautiful not in the exotic way of some women whose beauty depends on lighting, dress and circumstance. Debby is beautiful with the kind of beauty that makes people feel good about themselves. She is objectively beautiful — I mean beautiful in a photograph — but more. I keep trying not to say she glows because it's so cliched, but she does. Debby glows and she makes me glow. She is the soul of my bizarre and varied shell. She is the ground wire that makes it safe to operate, and she is the essence, the very center of what I am.

Debby, my childhood sweetheart.

Debby, the mother of our children.

I don't want to be away like this again. From now on we'll have these adventures as a couple.

It will be Debby and Brod in the glow of a kerosene lantern, awash in the imagined music of ''The Hall of the Mountain King...'' Debby and Brod on the glacier... Debby and Brod in the deepest reaches of the Amazon. Oh, she'll be overjoyed: ''Brod darling, did you catch a fever out there in all that ice?''

I also miss my guitar.

There is a lot of noise on 6th Street outside the Vance Hotel in the city of Seattle. There is just as much tonight as there was last night. But I don't seem to notice it as much tonight.

I'm ready to go home.

I have work to do, gifts to deliver, a new son to father and a wife worth living for.

Where is the suffering?

How will I ever be a great poet without the suffering?

ACKNOWLEDGEMENTS

Special thanks are due to the Caffin Avenue Poetry Society, for their friendship and support, and to Carol Rike, whose ear I wore smooth with the polishing of these poems. The Gustavus Inn is run by Joanne and Dave Lesh, who live on the premises with their beautiful children and set for their guests a table which rivals the great seafood restaurants of the world. Spirit Walker Expeditions is aptly named. Chief guide Greg Johns is a wilderness medium for whom the chill of ice is the touch of an old friend. I would also acknowledge mountain goat Mike Vales; wild man of the kayak Carlos Lincoln; beautiful Brenda Beeley; wilderness woman Kara Berg; green-eyed Katie Krathwohl; the tolerant Joanne and Grant Settlemier; and silent Neil Gende. Thanks also to Barbara Harding, who reads ''final'' copy with the eye of a jeweler, and to Nick Marinello for his sound sense of design.

About The Author

Brod Bagert is a trial lawyer in the city of New Orleans, where he once served as a member of the City Council. He is married, has four children, has not yet gone to Peru (please send airline tickets), and likes to get letters from strangers.

About The Artist

Stephen Morillo is a professor of medieval history, a Rhodes Scholar, artist, cricket player, and a glutton for punishment. This is his second book with Brod.